How to Make Money from your Blog by Blogging to a Book

Tips to help you Confront Your Finances, Reduce Your Expenses and Increase Your Income

Richard G Lowe, Jr

How to Make Money from your Blog by Blogging to a Book

Tips to help you Confront Your Finances, Reduce Your Expenses and Increase Your Income

Professional Freelance Writer Series #3

Published by The Writing King
www.thewritingking.com

How to Make Money from your Blog by Blogging to a Book

Cover Artist: theamateurzone

ASIN: B01KPIFIA8
ISBN: 978-1-943517-73-2 (Hardcover)
ISBN: 978-1-943517-72-5 (Paperback)
ISBN: 978-1-943517-40-4 (eBook)

Table of Contents

Introduction

For many people, their blog is their obsession. It is the way they communicate their thoughts and passions to the rest of the world. For these, making money off of a blog is not important; they want to get their message out, and cause people to understand what they have to say and to get positive feedback.

These blogs are gold mines of information about a particular subject, carefully written and organized to make everything easy to find and useful. They are often current, since they are written in the present, yet contain archives of old posts going back months, years, and in some cases decades.

For others, their blog is a means to an end. They want to promote their products, sell books, elect a political candidate, or make money from banners and advertisements. Or make money from banners and advertisements.

Regardless of the purpose of the blog and the motivation behind its creation, a lot of effort went in to writing the articles and other content. In many cases, those articles had to be researched, outlined, interviewed, written, proofread, and even reviewed by others for accuracy.

Wouldn't it be great if all that work could be reused in another form to make even more money or gain access to a wider audience?

You can repurpose those articles, assuming you own the copyrights, by compiling them into a book. Depending on the

Introduction

length of the articles, you could publish a collection of twenty, fifty or even a hundred of your blog posts into a very nice, insightful book.

Assuming the blog articles are well written, and your title, the description and book cover are well done, such a book could sell moderately well and make you some extra money.

Another reason for creating this kind of book is that you can publish it as a paperback, then order several copies which you use in public speaking engagements. These books can be sold "at the back of the room," and may also add to your credibility of the expert.

You have several options regarding the type of book to create. You can publish it as a short eBook, a paperback book, or a free download to get people to sign up for your email list. None of these options are mutually exclusive; there is no reason why you couldn't publish it as an e-book, a paperback, and a free download.

You can sell your book to make money; you can use it to establish credibility; or, as mentioned earlier, you can give it away as a free incentive to join your mailing list.

Publishing a book is one of the best ways to establish your credibility as an expert on the subject. People look up to authors, and it is assumed that by the very fact that a book was published the author knows what he's talking about.

There are several products, including WordPress plug-ins, that will read the posts from a blog and compile them into a book. In theory, this should make the effort of a blog-to-book project very simple. Unfortunately, books created using this method tend to be a very poor quality. A blog presents information in a different way than a book, and in order to work well the articles must be edited. If the blog-to-book project was not planned from the start, that editing project can be significant.

Each article will need to be modified and edited by hand to fit into the book and its theme. Content must be added to smoothly transition from article to article, and it all needs to be organized in such a way as to make sense. Other material such as a preface, introduction, conclusion and so on will need to be written.

The process is much easier if you plan to create a book from your blog from the beginning, since you can write each article with a book in mind.

Regardless, the effort to create the book is often worth the investment, if only to establish your credibility and enhance your personal brand.

Keep in mind that the effort to do this conversion can be outsourced to a ghostwriter, who can do most of the work for you. Since the content has already been written, the ghostwriter's job will be to convert it into a format suitable for publication as a book. Your job will be to review the contents and guide the ghostwriter to produce the book in the way that you want.

Introduction

I hope you enjoy what I've written and find it to be of some value. If you would like to send me a note about this book, feel free to write me at rich@thewritingking.com. If you enjoyed the book, please write a positive review.

Creating a Book from a Blog

Keep in mind, you should use your blog to promote your book while you are in the process of compiling the articles and working through the blog-to-book process. Once the book has been published, it can be used to promote the blog.

You have to remember, though, that the format, audience and intention of the two media are very different. If possible, you can do some planning up front to make the job of converting a blog into a marketable book much easier.

The best time to decide to blog-to-book is before you begin creating the blog. You can make this decision at any point, but if you write each article with the intention of creating a book, you will find makes the book compilation process much simpler. Otherwise, you will need to do a lot of editing to make all of the articles work together.

There are basically four different methods to create a book from a blog. These are listed below:

> ➢ Use a blog-to-book utility to lift the content from your blog and automatically create a book. This is the fastest method but creates the poorest quality book.
> ➢ Create a book from an existing blog and edit the book manuscript yourself. This produces a good finished quality book but requires more work since the manuscript was not planned from the beginning.
> ➢ Decide you want to blog to book before you start writing the blog. This is the optimum way to create a book from a blog as you can work towards the book as you write

the blog. All of the blog articles will then be targeted towards the end product of a book, requiring little editing at the time the manuscript is created.

➢ Hire a ghostwriter to write the blog articles and when complete use them to create a manuscript for your book. This method requires the least amount of work from you but obviously has a higher cost.

The process of blogging to a book is described in the following sections.

Pick a niche and an angle

The best bloggers don't write about everything under the sun, although, if you want, you can create a blog about a wide variety of subject. Many successful bloggers have taken that course of action. You could also blog about a different subject every week or just pick whatever is on your mind today and write about it online.

Unfortunately the scattershot approach of writing about everything doesn't attract a lot of readers, unless, of course, you are famous in your own right. Oprah might be able to get away with blogging about a different topic every day, but more than likely you will not have the same success.

The best and most popular blogs focus on a single subject, narrowly targetted on an area that the blogger knows well. In addition, good blogs find an angle or approach which is enticing and unique. For example, there are thousands of blogs about personal computers, and most of them don't get many visitors. But if you made a personal computer blog using cartoons or goofy stories you might have found a niche.

The point is to make your blog unique, give readers that extra reason not just to visit and come back, but to recommend your writing to friends and family. Once you've found that sweet spot, that beautiful niche that makes your blog unique, you'll find yourself getting more and more visitors. In fact, your biggest problem might turn out to be finding a web host powerful enough to handle your site!

Pick a niche and an angle

Now that you've got a blog which tells a story in a more-or-less unique way, you've got the beginnings of a book that has sales potential. Better still, you are creating an audience for that book: everyone who checks out the blog is a potential purchaser of your manuscript.

Hire a ghostwriter

One of the more interesting approaches to blogging combined with the idea of converting it into a book is to hire a ghostwriter. This relieves you of the effort to create your book and frees up your time to do other things.

The ghostwriter will help you by working with you to create an outline of your book and a plan to getting it completed. Once the outline is done and you have an idea of how large the book will be, you can come up with a projected publishing date. From there, you and the writer can work out how many articles to publish in your blog each month.

This often works very well financially as the budget can be spread out over the length of time it takes to write the blog articles. The rates can be very reasonable. Of course, once the articles have been written the ghostwriter can be engaged, on a separate contract, to pull all of that material together into a manuscript ready for publication.

What a ghostwriter does is take your ideas, concepts and opinions, and turn them into completed articles. By taking this approach you can be assured of getting quality articles without needing to spend the time and effort to write them yourself.

Create an outline

Whether you want to take an existing blog and turn it into a book or start from scratch, the first step, after figuring out the subject and niche, is to create an outline. One of the big differences between a book and a blog is blogs tend to be more random, while books have a structure that ties everything together.

The focus of the two formats is different. Each article within a blog is generally self-contained and doesn't usually flow in any particular direction. An entry one day may have absolutely nothing to do with one from last week, other than being loosely on the same subject. Readers may jump into a blog at any point, so each article needs to stand alone to a greater-or-lesser degree, although they can, of course, reference each other.

Books, on the other hand, have a more defined structure because they are read, for the most part, from front to back. They tend to follow an outline, have a chapter oriented format, and it can be anticipated that readers will follow with that format as they read.

Creating an outline for a blog will help you put the loose organization of a blog into the more rigid format of a book. If you create the outline before you begin blogging, you'll know exactly what you need to write and how it fits into the overall picture.

On the other hand, if you've already got a blog with many articles, the outline allows you to determine gaps and holes in

Create an outline

what you are trying to communicate. Those will become the blog entries you will want to write upon to finish the book. You may also find blog entries which don't fit well into your outline and need to be modified or discarded.

The outline determines the structure of the book, and it is absolutely critical in the process of creating strongly focused book of interest to your readers. It concentrates your writing efforts towards a particular goal to be reached by the time the reader closes the book at the end. This is the primary difference between a blog and a book.

Come up with a plan

Your outline is the start of the plan for your book. This gives you the structure and defines the areas you want to address in your text. The effort you spend on the outline is time well spent, as your book will be stronger because of it.

You must also think about your audience. Who are you talking to? The best books are written with a very well defined audience in mind and all of the words and phrases are aimed at them. With a blog you have a little more freedom to deviate from your intended audience, since the articles are generally not read in order; visitors may arrive at any article at random.

A book is typically sold on bookstore websites, and they are targeted toward a specific audience. Your audience might be children, parents, working single moms, bored teenagers, doctors, lawyers or whatever. Choose your audience and ensure your blog (and future book) articles are written towards that audience.

Decide if you want to write the book in order, from front to back, in your blog, or if you are going to randomly write and post articles online. There are advantages to either approach. I prefer writing the articles in order since it fits more into the book format. Of course if you've already been writing articles for your blog this decision has already been made.

Now think about when you want that book to be ready for market. This is very important as blogs tend to go on forever while books are published and have definite milestones. If your outline has fifty sections and you want to do one blog

Come up with a plan

entry a week, that's about a year before you start the book making (as opposed to the book writing) period.

Your projected end date will help you determine how many articles you will publish in your blog over what time period. Remember you are going to need some time to touch up those blog entries to make them suitable for publication. Be sure to factor that into your schedule.

Remember copyright laws. This is very important. Be sure not to plagiarize anything and always cite your sources. This is different from a blog where you can just include a link to an online source. Include hyperlinks to online sources, but you should still create a bibliography of all source materials.

You must include a citation to any sources you reference. Microsoft Word has an excellent citation tool built in to make this easy.

Write your blog entries

Using your outline as a guide, write your blog articles or write the ones that are missing. Now that you've decided to create a book from the blog you can focus more on making the articles suitable for publication. Keep your audience in mind, and fit each blog entry into your overall outline and plan.

One strategy which can be used very well in promoting the book is to let your readers know more information will be available in the book. So you might write each blog article at 750 words, but when you edit them into a final manuscript expand them to double the size with more information or quotes or whatever else you'd like. This gives the readers of your blog incentive to purchase the book.

You can do the same thing in reverse. The finished book can reference the blog, citing it for additional information or articles that were not included in the book. Thus the book and blog can be used to promote each other.

Edit your blog into a manuscript

Once you've written all of the blog articles you need for your book, it is time to edit them into a manuscript. If you had a good plan and wrote your articles according to that plan this should not be a lengthy process.

It is a mistake to use one of the supposedly "quick and easy" blog-to-book services or products. These tools have their place, but creating a publishable, marketable and high quality manuscript is not their forte. Sure they are quick and they do let you create a book, but it's not going to be very useful. You could use these tools to publish it as an eBook, but I think you'll be disappointed with the results.

You should think of your blog as a draft copy of your book. You will need to do a lot of editing and more than a few revisions to produce a quality manuscript.

Copy the text of each article from the blog into your word processor. I've found it best to complete each article one at a time rather than attempting to copy them in all at once. Working on them one by one creates more bite-sized chunks, which I have found to be easier to work on.

Any hyperlinks will have to be removed (unless the format is eBook) and, if needed, added as citations or footnotes.

Spend the time to edit each article, fitting it into your outline and working it to further the purpose of the book. You should look out for articles (especially if they were written before you decided to create a book from your blog) which do not

Edit your blog into a manuscript

communicate to the right audience. These will need to be edited so they work as part of your book.

Some articles will need quite a bit of editing and others will require a minor amount of effort. Don't be concerned about the effort involved. Just edit each article to fit into your book, and aim towards creating high quality.

Keep in mind that the articles on your blog do not need to match the articles in your book. In fact, the book will be more useful if it deviates to a greater or lesser degree from your blog.

Since blogs are generally written more in present time than books, you should be on the lookout for obsolete information. Correct or discard these as needed.

A nice feature of blogs is the fact that readers can leave comments. You can use those comments, either via direct quotes or by paraphrasing, in selected places within your book. This can add the thoughts and opinions of others and make the book more interesting.

Once you've got all of your articles converted over to manuscript format and they have been edited to fit into the book, reread the whole thing from front to back, then read it again. Leave a few days between each reading. Once you've been through the book at least twice, read it out loud. I am always amazed at how many errors that simple step can catch.

To make your book truly professional submit it to be edited by an editor. By this I mean a real-live, professional editor. You can find editing services online who have people on staff who will find grammar, spelling and typing errors for you. This can make the difference between an excellent book and one that screams amateur. A website called Fiverr is an excellent place to find good proofreaders for low cost. I've had excellent results from Robinoo, who does both copy editing and proofreading.

Don't forget to send your manuscript to a few people to review for accuracy. Their job is to find any technical errors and give you feedback about readability, consistency and missing information. Friends, family members, co-workers and colleagues are a great source for these reviews. One good way to entice colleagues to review a book is to offer them the same services for their own books when they publish.

Promote your book

As you are writing your blog, intending to convert it into a manuscript down the road, be sure to promote the "up-and-coming" book. Get your readers excited by including quotes and excerpts. You could even allow the book to be bought at a lesser price in advance of publication.

Remember to use more than your blog for promotion. Social media sites such as LinkedIn and Facebook, and online forums, are also great places to build excitement.

As I pointed out earlier, blog articles can reference the book for more information. Your promotion efforts should reinforce that your book contains updated information, additional articles or other features not available online.

Another thing you can do is create short articles that summarize sections of your book, or add additional quotes, humor, graphics or other similar items to the book. This gives your blog readers still more reason to want to purchase your book.

Note this can work both ways. Your book can also reference sections of the blog for expanded information, additional resources or more current coverage.

A final point to keep in mind is to use the blog and the book to promote your next book. Drop some hints as to the content and give your readers something to look forward to

Conclusions

Creating a book from a blog, a book which will be published and sold, can be a very rewarding experience. In many ways blogging is easier than the writing an actual manuscript, since the large commitment of time is spread out over a long period. Blogs also get regular and immediate feedback, something that is missing while writing a book.

The best thing about using your blog content to publish a book is that much of the work is already been done. Articles which have already been written can be repurposed, usually with a little bit of editing, into a successful book which helps brand you and give you credibility. Anyone can create a blog, but only a few people, in comparison, have gone so far as to publish a book.

The best thing you can do when you start your blog is to write your articles with an eye towards publishing a book at a later date. By doing this, you can write your text in such a way that there is minimal editing later on. Otherwise, your editing task will be larger because you have to create transitions from article to article.

In any event, the task of publishing a book from your blog can be very fulfilling and, depending on the subject, could the very lucrative. Since publishing is free on many publishing sites, there is no reason not to at least compile your articles into a published book.

Conclusions

Before you go

If you scroll to the last page in this eBook, you will have the opportunity to leave feedback and share the book with Before You Go. I'd be grateful if you turned to the last page and shared the book.

Also, if you have time, please leave a review. Positive reviews are incredibly useful. If you didn't like the book, please email me at rich@thewritingking.com and I'd be happy to get your input.

linkedin.thewritingking.com

About the Author

https://www.linkedin.com/in/richardlowejr
Feel free to send a connection request

Follow me on Twitter: @richardlowejr

Richard Lowe has leveraged more than 35 years of experience as a Senior Computer Manager and Designer at four companies into that of a bestselling author, blogger, ghostwriter, and public speaker. He has written hundreds of articles for blogs and ghostwritten more than a dozen books and has published manuscripts about computers, the Internet, surviving disasters, management, and human rights. He is currently working on a ten-volume science fiction series – the Peacekeeper Series – to be published at the rate of three volumes per year, beginning in 2016.

Richard started in the field of Information Technology, first as the Vice President of Consulting at Software Techniques, Inc. Because he craved action, after six years he moved on to work for two companies at the same time: he was the Vice President of Consulting at Beck Computer Systems and the Senior Designer at BIF Accutel. In January 1994, Richard found a home at Trader Joe's as the Director of Technical Services and Computer Operations. He remained with that incredible company for almost 20 years before taking an early retirement to begin a new life as a professional writer. He is currently the CEO of The Writing King, a company that provides all forms of writing services, the owner of The EBay King, and a Senior Branding Expert for LinkedIn Makeover. You can find a current list of all books on his Author Page and

About the Author

take a look at his exclusive line of coloring books at The Coloring King.

Richard has a quirky sense of humor and has found that life is full of joy and wonder. As he puts it, "This little ball of rock, mud, and water we call Earth is an incredible place, with many secrets to discover. Beings fill our corner of the universe, and some are happy, and others are sad, but each has their unique story to tell."

His philosophy is to take life with a light heart, and he approaches each day as a new source of happiness. Evil is ignored, discarded, or defeated; good is helped, enriched, and fulfilled. One of his primary interests is to educate people about their human rights and assist them to learn how to be happy in life.

Richard spent many happy days hiking in national parks, crawling over boulders, and peering at Indian pictographs. He toured the Channel Islands off Santa Barbara and stared in fascination at wasps building their homes in Anza-Borrego. One of his joys is photography, and he has photographed more than 1,200 belly dancing events, as well as dozens of Renaissance fairs all over the country.

Because writing is his passion, Richard remains incredibly creative and prolific; each day he writes between 5,000 and 10,000 words, diligently using language to bring life to the world so that others may learn and be entertained.

Richard is the CEO of The Writing King, which specializes in fulfilling any writing need. You can find out more at https://www.thewritingking.com/, and emails are welcome at rich@thewritingking.com

Books by Richard G Lowe Jr.

Business Professional Series

On the Professional Code of Ethics and Business Conduct in the Workplace – Professional Ethics: 100 Tips to Improve Your Professional Life - have you ever wondered what it takes to be successful in the professional world? This book gives you some tips that will improve your job and your career.

Help! My Boss is Whacko! - How to Deal with a Hostile Work Environment - sometimes the problem is the boss. There are all kinds of managers, some competent, some incompetent, and others just plain whacked. This book will help you understand and handle those different types of managers.

Help! I've Lost My Job: Tips on What to do When You're Unexpectedly Unemployed – suddenly having to leave your job can be a harsh and emotional time in your life. Learn some of the things that you need to consider and handle if this happens to you.

Help! My Job Sucks Insider Tips on Making Your Job More Satisfying and Improving Your Career – sometimes conditions conspire to make the regular trek to a job feel like a trip through Dante's Inferno. Sometimes, these are out of our control, such as a malicious manager or incompetent colleague. On the other hand, we can take control of our lives and workplace and improve our situation. Get this book to learn what you can do when your job sucks.

Books by Richard G Lowe Jr.

How to Manage a Consulting Project: Make money, get your project done on time, and get referred again and again – I found that being a consultant is a great way to earn a living. Managing a consulting project can be a challenge. This book contains some tips to help you so you can deliver a better product or service to your customers.

How to be a Good Manager and Supervisor, and How to Delegate – Lessons Learned from the Trenches: Insider Secrets for Managers and Supervisors – I've been a manager for over thirty years I learned many things about how to get the job done and deliver quality service. The information in this book will help you manage your projects to a high level of quality.

Focus on LinkedIn – Learn how to create a LinkedIn profile and to network effectively using the #1 business social media site.

Home Computer Security Series

Safe Computing is Like Safe Sex: You have to practice it to avoid infection – Security expert and Computer Executive, Richard Lowe, presents the simple steps you can take to protect your computer, photos and information from evil doers and viruses. Using easy-to-understand examples and simple explanations, Lowe explains why hackers want your system, what they do with your information, and what you can do to keep them at bay. Lowe answers the question: how to you keep yourself say in the wild west of the internet.

Books by Richard G Lowe Jr.

Disaster Preparation and Survival Series

Real World Survival Tips and Survival Guide: Preparing for and Surviving Disasters with Survival Skills – CERT (Civilian Emergency Response Team) trained and Disaster Recovery Specialist, Richard Lowe, lays out how to make you, your family, and your friends ready for any disaster, large or small. Based upon specialized training, interviews with experts and personal experience, Lowe answers the big question: what is the secret to improving the odds of survival even after a big disaster?

Creating a Bug Out Bag to Save Your Life: What you need to pack for emergency evacuations - When you are ordered to evacuate—or leave of your free will—you probably won't have a lot of time to gather your belongings and the things you'll need. You may have just a few minutes to get out of your home. The best preparation for evacuation is to create what is called a bug out bag. These are also known as go-bags, as in, "grab it and go!"

Professional Freelance Writer Series

How to Operate a Freelance Writing Business, and How to be a Ghostwriter – Proven Tips and Tricks Every Author Needs to Know about Freelance Writing: Insider Secrets from a Professional Ghostwriter – This book explains how to be a ghostwriter, and gives tips on everything from finding customers to creating a statement of work to delivering your final product.

How to Write a Blog That Sells and How to Make Money From Blogging: Insider Secrets from a Professional Blogger:

Books by Richard G Lowe Jr.

Proven Tips and Tricks Every Blogger Needs to Know to Make Money – There is an art to writing an article that prompts the reader to make a decision to do something. That's the narrow focus of this book. You will learn how to create an article that gets a reader interested, entices them, informs them, and causes them to make a decision when they reach the end.

<u>Other Books by Richard Lowe Jr</u>

<u>How to Be Friends with Women: How to Surround Yourself with Beautiful Women without Being Sleazy</u> – I am a photographer and frequently find myself surrounded by some of the most beautiful women in the world. This book explains how men can attract women and keep them as friends, which can often lead to real, fulfilling relationships.

<u>How to Throw Parties like a Professional: Tips to Help You Succeed with Putting on a Party Event</u> – Many of us have put on parties, and I know it can be a daunting and confusing experience. In this book, I share what I learned from hosting small house parties to shows and events.

Additional Resources

Is your career important to you? Find out how to move your career in any direction you desire, improve your long-term livelihood, and be prepared for any eventuality. Visit the page below to sign up to receive valuable tips via email, and to get a free eBook about how to optimize your LinkedIn profile.

http://list.thewritingking.com/

I've written and published many books on a variety of subjects. They are all listed on the following page.

https://www.thewritingking.com/books/

On that site, I also publish articles about business, writing, and other subjects. You can visit by clicking the following link:

https://www.thewritingking.com

To find out more about me or my photography, you can visit these sites:

Personal website: https://www.richardlowe.com
Photography: http://www.richardlowejr.com
LinkedIn Profile: https://www.linkedin.com/in/richardlowejr
Twitter: https://twitter.com/richardlowejr

If you have any comments about this book, feel free to email me at rich@thewritingking.com

Premium Writing Services

Do you have a story that needs to be told? Have you been trying to write a book for ages but never can seem to find the time to get it done? Do you want to brand your business, but don't know how to get started?

The Writing King has the answer. We can help you with any of your writing needs.

Ghostwriting. We can write your book, which entails interviewing you to get your story, writing the book and then working with you to revise it until complete. To discuss your book, contact The Writing King today.

Website Copy. Many businesses include the text on their sites as an afterthought, and that can result in lost sales and leads. Hire The Writing King to review your site and recommend changes to the text which will help communicate your message and improve your sales.

Blogging. Build engagement with your customers by hiring us to write a weekly or semi-weekly article for your blog, LinkedIn or other social media. Contact The Writing King today to discuss your blogging needs.

LinkedIn. LinkedIn is of the most important vehicles for finding new business, and a professionally written profile works to pulling in those leads. Write or update your profile today.

Technical Writing. We have broad experience in the computer, warehousing and retail industries, and have

Premium Writing Services

written hundreds of technical documents. Contact The Writing King today to find out how we can help you with your technical writing project.

The Writing King has the skills and knowledge to help you with any of your writing needs. Call us today to discuss how we can help you.